The
Experience
of
prayer

Volumes in the Pathway to the Heart of God Series

The Experience of Prayer
The Journey of Prayer
The Joy of Prayer
A Time for Prayer

PATHWAY TO THE HEART OF GOD

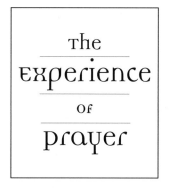

The
Experience
of
prayer

TERRY W. GLASPEY

Cumberland House Publishing
Nashville, Tennessee

Published by Cumberland House Publishing, Inc., 431 Harding Industrial Drive, Nashville, Tennessee 37211

Unless otherwise indicated, verses are taken from the Holy Bible, New International Version ®, Copyright © 1973, 1978, 1984 by the International Bible Society. Used by permission of Zondervan Publishing House. The "NIV" and "New International Version" trademarks are registered in the United States Patent and Trademark Office by the International Bible Society.

Verses marked NASB are taken from the New American Standard Bible, © 1960, 1962, 1963, 1968, 1971, 1972, 1973, 1975, 1977 by The Lockman Foundation. Used by permission.

Verses marked NRSV are taken from The New Revised Standard Version of the Bible (NRSV), copyright © 1989 by the Division of Christian Education of the National Council of the Churches of Christ in the USA. Used by permission. All rights reserved.

Cover design by Karen Phillips
Text design by Julia M. Pitkin

Library of Congress Cataloging-in-Publication Data

Glaspey, Terry W.
    The experience of prayer / Terry W. Glaspey.
        p. cm. -- (Pathway to the heart of God series)
    ISBN: 1-58182-134-4 (alk. paper)
    1. Prayer--Christianity. 2. Prayer--Christianity--Quotations, maxims, etc. I. Title.

BV215.G57 2000
248.3'2--dc21   00-058988

Printed in the United States of America
1 2 3 4 5 6 7 8 — 05 04 03 02 01 00

contents

Introduction

I suppose that nearly everyone feels that they should pray. But why is it that so few of us actually do pray in any consistent manner? Why do we leave such an important element of our spiritual lives to the whim of our harried schedules?

Could it be that we do not pray with regularity because we really don't know where to start? That we lack the understanding of the nuts and bolts involved in improving our personal experience of prayer? In the pages that follow, we'll see what we can learn from some of the great pray-ers of the past, the saints whose lives were transformed by their prayers. They will give us valuable insights into how we can make powerful prayer a part of our spiritual lives. They will help us to take the next step.

The little book you hold in your hand is the fourth of four little books about prayer. This particular volume is focused upon on providing practical steps for beginning to make prayer a more integral part of our lives. The other books in the series look at what prayer really is and how God uses it so powerfully in our lives (*A Time for Prayer*), examine the different elements of a balanced prayer life (*The Joy of Prayer*), and wrestle with some of the tough questions we all have about prayer (*The Journey of Prayer*). Each of the four books is a part of the whole. Taken together, their goal is not only to help us understand prayer a little better, but also to inspire us to begin to pray.

Prayer is a topic that continues to be much discussed these days, especially by those who are concerned with making sense of their spiritual lives. There are lots of books around that attempt to explain the ins and outs of what prayer is and how it affects one's life. Some of them claim to have all the answers, to have unlocked some secret key or system for making prayer effective for the reader.

I make no such claim. Like you, I am a learner in the school of prayer. But one of the important things I have learned is that I am not on my own when it comes to making sense of this crucial element of my spiritual life. Many great thinkers, writers, theologians, mystics, and activists have ruminated deeply on this important topic. In this book, I hope to share a little of what I've learned from them, mostly in their own words. If, like me, you realize you have a lot to learn and you truly desire to make your prayer life more meaningful, then I invite you to join me in meditating on some of the most profound and life-changing words ever written about prayer.

Each year brings a multitude of new books on prayer. One of the lessons I have learned about such books is that the most recent ones are not necessarily the best ones. It seems that a lot of books published these days are tainted with our modern, materialistic values or our current obsession with the therapeutic sphere. Such books tend to be more concerned with using prayer as a way to get what we want or as a method for obtaining inner peace and tranquility than with learning how to make communication with God a part of our everyday existence and with growing into a more intimate relationship with Him.

I invite you, then, to join me on a journey that will sample the thoughts of some of the most insightful believers who ever lived (along with a handful of nonbelievers who thought deeply about the subject). These nuggets of wisdom are best absorbed thoughtfully and slowly, a few at a time. If we are to enter the school of prayer, we must not rush to consider ourselves graduates. Savor these thoughts. Meditate on them. Argue with them. Make them your own.

The writers quoted in this book come from a variety of time periods, religious traditions, cultures, and life experiences. Be forewarned: They do not always agree with each other. Most of the time I have simply allowed their disagreements to stand, expecting the reader to ponder their thoughts with discernment and draw his or her own conclusions. At other times, I have tried to synthesize the various insights together, still endeavoring to avoid the temptation of superficially explaining away the mysteries that will always surround this topic.

Sprinkled in with the text you'll also find some of my favorite prayers from classic writers, many of them composed by the same writers whose thoughts on prayer we will consider. You can use these prayers as models to fashion your own, as inspiration to prepare your heart to pray, or as a way to give voice to concerns and feelings you cannot articulate as well as these saints. You and I can make these prayers our own, for often they can help us express what we would struggle to put into words for ourselves. When prayed with focus and concentration, they can give our hearts wings to fly upward to God.

Finally, I have concluded each section of this book with a prayer I have written. These little prayers are attempts to put the truths of the chapter into practice…for it does us little good to think about prayer or read about praying if we don't actually pray.

I hope you will find this little book to be a helpful companion as you travel your own spiritual path. Think of it as a map you can use as you begin your personal journey into God's heart.

Terry W. Glaspey

The
Experience
of
prayer

LEARNING TO LISTEN

Sometimes we make the mistake of thinking of prayer as a monologue. We consider only our part in the conversation. We talk to God, letting Him know our needs and desires. But true conversation does not take place when only one party is speaking. It takes two people to have a conversation, and if prayer is a conversation, we ought to learn to listen as well as speak. We should not be content with filling the air with our words. We must also attune our ears to listen, for God desires to speak to His children.

Because God longs to have relationship with His people, prayer is not a formal exercise, but an experience of real communication. He is not only the God who hears, but also the God who speaks. If we listen closely, we will sense direction, encouragement, rebuke, or whatever it may be that He yearns to say to us.

Of course we are not listening for an audible voice. Instead of a voice that rises from vocal chords, we listen for one that arises from the quiet depths of the heart. An important part of the art of prayer is learning to quiet ourselves so that we can actually hear His voice in the tumult of our lives. Our circumstances, our selfish desires, our fantasies and dreams, the confusing advice of others—all these work to drown out His call to us. We must prepare ourselves to listen, for it is in a gentle whisper, not a thunderous voice, that God usually chooses to speak to us.

The word of the LORD came to him:
"What are you doing here, Elijah?" He replied,
"I have been very zealous for the LORD God
Almighty. The Israelites have rejected your covenant,
broken down your altars, and put your prophets to
death with the sword. I am the only one left, and
now they are trying to kill me too." Then the LORD
said, "Go out and stand on the mountain in the
presence of the LORD, for the LORD is about to pass
by." Then a great and powerful wind tore the
mountains apart and shattered the rocks before
the LORD, but the LORD was not in the wind.
After the wind there was an earthquake, but the
LORD was not in the earthquake. After the
earthquake came a fire…. And after the fire
came a gentle whisper. When Elijah heard it,
he pulled his cloak over his face and went
out and stood at the mouth of the cave.
—I KINGS 19:9-13

*Talkativeness is the throne of vainglory
on which it loves to preen itself and show off.
Talkativeness is a sign of ignorance, a doorway
to slander, a leader of jesting, a servant of lies, the
ruin of compunction, a summoner of despondency,
a messenger of sleep, a dissipation of recollection,
the end of vigilance, the cooling of zeal, the
darkening of prayer. Intelligent silence is
the mother of prayer, freedom from
bondage, custodian of zeal,
a guard on our thoughts.*
—JOHN CLIMACUS

*The LORD is in his holy temple;
let all the earth keep silence before him.*
—HABBAKUK 2:20

My soul, wait in silence for God only,
For my hope is from Him.
He is my rock and my salvation.
My stronghold, I shall not be shaken.
—PSALM 62:5,6 NASB

I always begin my prayer in silence,
for it is in the silence of the heart that
God speaks. God is the friend of silence—
we need to listen to God because it's not
what we say but what He says to
us and through us that matters.
—MOTHER TERESA

Prayer at its highest is a two-way conversation—
and for me the most important part is
listening to God's replies.
—FRANK C. LAUBACH

Be silent, and listen to God.
Let your heart be in such a state of
preparation that His Spirit may impress
upon you such virtues as will please Him.
Let all within you listen to Him. This silence
of all outward and earthly affection and of
human thoughts within us is essential
if we are to hear His voice.
—FRANÇOIS FÉNELON

God never ceases to speak to us:
but the noise of the world without,
and the tumult of our passions within,
bewilder us, and prevent us
from listening to Him.
—FRANCOIS FÉNELON

Prayer is not to hear oneself speak,
but to arrive at silence, and continue being silent:
to wait till one hears God speak.
—SÖREN KIERKEGAARD

Prayer is not monologue, but dialogue;
God's voice in response to mine is its most essential
part. Listening to God's voice is the secret of the
assurance that He will listen to mine.
—ANDREW MURRAY

We must silence every creature,
we must silence ourselves, to hear in the
deep hush of the whole soul, the ineffable voice
of the spouse. We must bend the ear, because
it is a gentle and delicate voice, only heard
by those who no longer hear anything else.
—FRANÇOIS FÉNELON

A man prayed, and at first
he thought that prayer was talking.
But he became more and more quiet
until in the end he realized that
prayer is listening.
—SÖREN KIERKEGAARD

Silence is not easy. It goes against many of our natural inclinations.

Do not be afraid of silence
in your prayer time. It may be that
you are meant to listen, not to speak. So
wait before the Lord. Wait in stillness. Wait
as David waited when he "sat before the LORD."
And in that stillness, assurance will come to you.
You will know that you are heard; you will
know that your Lord ponders the voice of
your humble desires; you will hear quiet
words spoken to you yourself, perhaps to
your grateful surprise and refreshment.
—AMY CARMICHAEL

As soon as we are alone,
without people to talk with, books to read,
TV to watch, or phone calls to make, an inner
chaos opens up in us....This chaos can be so
disturbing and so confusing that we can
hardly wait to get busy again.
—HENRI J. M. NOUWEN

However difficult it may sound,
the hearing really precedes the asking.
It is the basis of it. It makes it real asking,
the asking of Christian prayer.
—KARL BARTH

I do not know it and do not understand it,
but sounding from above and ringing in my ears
I hear what is beyond the thought of man.
—MARTIN LUTHER

*Learn to abide with attention in loving
waiting upon God in the state of quiet;
give no heed to your imagination, nor to
its operations, for now, as I have said,
the powers of the soul are at rest
and are not exercised except in the
sweet and pure waiting of love.*
—JOHN OF THE CROSS

*Prayer begins by talking to God,
but it ends by listening to Him.*
—FULTON SHEEN

*Hasten unto him who calls you
in the silences of your heart.*
—THOMAS KELLY

*Solitude and silence can never be
separated from the call to unceasing prayer.
If solitude were primarily an escape from a busy
job, and silence primarily an escape from a noisy
milieu, they could easily become very self-centered
forms of asceticism. But solitude and silence are for
prayer. The Desert Fathers did not think of solitude
as being alone, but as being alone with God. They
did not think of silence as not speaking, but as
listening to God. Solitude and silence are the
context within which prayer is practiced.*
—HENRI J. M. NOUWEN

*Come, Lord, and speak to my heart.
Communicate to it Your holy will, and mercifully
work within it both to will and to do
according to Your good pleasure.*
—THOMAS À KEMPIS

Lord, teach me to listen.
The times are noisy and my ears are
weary with the thousand raucous sounds
which continuously assault them. Give me the
spirit of the boy Samuel when he said to Thee,
"Speak for thy servant heareth." Let me hear
Thee speaking in my heart. Let me get used
to the sound of Thy voice, that its tones may
be familiar when the sounds of the earth
die away and the only sound will be the
music of Thy speaking voice. Amen.
—A. W. TOZER

Be still, and know that I am God.
—PSALM 46: 10

Lord,
I confess that I am often so caught up in
finding my own solutions
That I neglect to listen to you.
In a world where only the loud and the
well-publicized get heard,
I seldom am able to quiet my heart
Enough to hear your quiet wisdom.
Teach me, Lord,
To slow down,
To quiet down,
To find the gentle peace of your presence,
And hear your voice.
Amen.

PRACTICING THE
PRESENCE OF GOD

A turning point in my own prayer life came when I discovered a small book entitled *The Practice of the Presence of God*. It opened my eyes to a simple but powerful form of prayer: the usually wordless prayer of presence. This form of praying consists of simply placing ourselves in the presence of God and enjoying the fellowship of close intimacy with Him.

Brother Lawrence, a seventeenth-century monk, was not a great spiritual leader in his day. In fact, he had the rather unheralded job of working in the monastery kitchen. But he was a man who fervently desired to draw closer to God and longed for a deeper relationship with Him, one that went beyond the devotional acts required of him as a monk. He was not satisfied with the occasional religious ecstasy that came through performing the required religious duties, but wanted to learn to

dwell habitually in God's presence. Eventually, his
eyes were opened to the reality that we are always
in God's presence, even when we are not aware of
it. The conclusion he reached, though, was that
our consciousness of this fact will change our lives.
Therefore, amidst the clutter and clatter of the
kitchen, while he cooked and cleaned, he learned
to experience the reality of God's presence. He
writes of this experience—in the second person—
in *The Practice of the Presence of God*.

I know a person who for forty years
has practiced the presence of God intellectually
but gives it several other names; sometimes he calls
it a simple act or a clear and distinct knowledge of
God; at other times an indistinct vision or a loving
gaze, a sense of God, still other times he calls it a
waiting on God, a silent conversation with God,
trust in God, the life and peace of the soul; finally
this person told me that all of these [are]
expressions for the presence of God.

By force of habit and by frequently calling his
mind to the presence of God, he has developed
such a habit that as soon as he is free from his
external affairs, and even often while he is immersed
in them, the very heart of his soul, with no effort on
his part, is raised up above all things and stays
suspended and held there in God.

—BROTHER LAWRENCE

What can be more agreeable to God
than to withdraw thus many times a day
from the things of man to retire into ourselves
and adore Him interiorly?
—BROTHER LAWRENCE

We can achieve this sense of God's presence by surrendering our hearts and wills to Him, and through the conscious choice to make ourselves aware of Him throughout the day. We can learn to pray simultaneously with the other activities of our days, letting prayer season everything we do. If practiced regularly in this manner, prayer becomes as natural and integral to us as drawing our next breath.

*[We should] make a private chapel
of our heart where we can retire from time
to time to commune with Him, peacefully,
humbly, lovingly.*
—BROTHER LAWRENCE

*I keep myself in His presence
by simple attentiveness and a
loving gaze upon God.*
—BROTHER LAWRENCE

*Remember to retire occasionally into the
solitude of your heart while you are outwardly
engaged in business or conversation....Withdraw,
then, your thoughts, from time to time, into your
heart, where, separated from all men, you
may familiarly treat with God on the
affairs of your soul.*
—FRANCIS DE SALES

Brother Lawrence referred often to what he called "the interior gaze," a conscious turning of our heart and mind toward God on many occasions throughout the course of the day. This, of course, is yet another way of "praying without ceasing."

By the presence of God and by this
interior gaze, the soul comes to know God
in such a way that it passes almost all its
life in making continual acts of love, adoration,
contrition, trust, actions of grace, offering, petition,
and of all the most excellent virtues; and sometimes
it even becomes one endless act because the
soul is always engaged in staying in
this divine presence.
—BROTHER LAWRENCE

In modern times Frank Laubach, inspired by the example of Brother Lawrence, spoke of a similar experience. He kept a journal to record his endeavor to keep himself aware of God's presence in His life throughout every day.

*Yesterday and today I have made
a new adventure, which is not easy to express.
I am feeling God in each movement, by an act of
will—willing that He shall direct these fingers that
now strike this typewriter—willing that He shall
pour through my steps as I walk-willing that
He shall direct my words as I speak, and
my very jaws as I eat!*
—FRANK C. LAUBACH

*Oh, this thing of keeping in constant
touch with God, making Him the object of my
thought and the companion of my conversations,
is the most amazing thing I ever ran across.
It is working.*
—FRANK C. LAUBACH

So, let us strive to be conscious of God's presence in our lives, and let it bring us hope, comfort,
and transformation.

*Where can I go from your spirit?
Or where can I flee from your presence?
If I ascend to heaven, you are there,
if I make my bed in Sheol, you are there.
If I take the wings of morning and settle
at the farthest limits or the sea,
Even there your hand shall lead me,
and your right hand shall hold me fast.*
—PSALM 139:7-10, NRSV

*The holiest, most common, most necessary
practice of the spiritual life is the presence of God,
that is to take delight in and become accustomed to
His divine company, speaking humbly and talking
lovingly with Him at all times, at every moment,
without rule or system and especially in times of
temptation, suffering, spiritual aridity, disgust
and even of unfaithfulness and sin.*
— BROTHER LAWRENCE

*We pray to God. We speak to Him
about everything we have on our minds
both concerning others and ourselves. There
come times, not so seldom with me at least, when I
have nothing more to tell God. If I were to continue to
pray in words, I would have to repeat what I have
already said. At such times it is wonderful to say
to God, "May I be in Thy presence, Lord? I
have nothing more to say to Thee, but
I do love to be in Thy presence."*
— O. HALLESBY

Dear god,
of all the gifts you have given me,
perhaps the most precious is
your presence with me.
It fills me with joy and awe
when I consider that you have chosen
my unworthy heart as a dwelling place.
Keep me aware of your nearness
And remind me that I am

Never,

Never,

Never alone.

−3−
GROWING THROUGH
PRAYER

If God is all-powerful, then why do we need to pray? What is the point of making requests when He already knows all things, including what we need?

These are the kinds of questions we frequently ponder in our minds. But the great writers on prayer remind us that we pray not so much for God's sake as for our own. Not to let Him know, but to let ourselves be known.

Prayer not only changes things; it also changes us. It is an integral part of God's plan for our spiritual growth.

*Why does the Lord urge us to pray,
when He knows what we need before we
ask Him? This can seem puzzling, and can
make prayer seem like wasted effort. But prayer
is not merely expressing our present desires. Its
purpose is to exercise and train our desires, so that
we want what He is preparing to give. His gift is
very great, and we are small vessels for receiving it.
So prayer involves widening our hearts to God. We
pray to God at fixed times of the day in order to
remember our desire for God, And we pray in
words, which in themselves are mere symbols,
in order to focus our hearts on the inner
truths behind the words.*
—AUGUSTINE

*No matter how much our interior progress is
ordered, nothing will come of it unless by divine
aid. Divine aid is available to those who seek it
from their hearts, humbly and devoutly; and
this means to sigh for it, in this valley of
tears, through fervent prayer.*
—BONAVENTURE

Be not forgetful of prayer. Every time
you pray, if your prayer is sincere, there will be
a new feeling and a new meaning in it, which
will give you fresh courage, and you will
understand that prayer is an education.
—FYODOR DOSTOEVSKY

Let us then press on in prayer,
looking upwards to the divine benignant rays,
even as if a resplendent cord were hanging from
the height of heaven unto this world below, and we,
by seizing it with alternate hands in one advance,
appeared to pull it down; but in very truth instead
of drawing down the rope—the same being
already near us above and below, we were
ourselves being drawn upwards to
the higher refulgence of the
resplendent rays.
—DIONYSIUS THE AREOPAGITE

Prayer does not change God,
but changes him who prays.
—SÖREN KIERKEGAARD

*This mental prayer is of all others
the most effectual to purify the soul, and
dispose it unto a holy and religious temper,
and may be termed the great secret of devotion
and one of the most powerful instruments
of the divine life.*
—HENRY SCOUGAL

*The prayer preceding all prayers is
"May it be the real I who speaks. May it be
the real Thou that I speak to." Infinitely various
are the levels from which we pray. Emotional
intensity is in itself no proof of spiritual depth. If
we pray in terror we shall pray earnestly; it only
proves that terror is an earnest emotion. Only God
Himself can let the bucket down to the depths in us.
And, on the other side, He must constantly work as
the iconoclast. Every idea of Him we form, He must
in mercy shatter. The most blessed result of prayer
would be to rise thinking "But I never knew before,
I never dreamed.…" I suppose it was at such a
moment that Thomas Aquainas said of all his
own theology, "It reminds me of straw."*
—C. S. LEWIS

Prayer is, indeed, one of the most important factors in our spiritual growth. It can be said with absolute certainty that Christians who pray are Christians who experience spiritual growth.

I have read the lives of many eminent Christians who have been on earth since the Bible days. Some of them, I see, were rich, and some poor. Some were learned, some unlearned. Some of them were Episcopalians, and some Christians of other denominations. Some were Calvinists, and some were Arminians. Some have loved to use a liturgy, and some chose to use none. But one thing, I see, they all had in common. They all have been men of prayer.

—J. C. RYLE

*Let us be careful to consider not only
the length of time we spend with God in prayer,
but the power with which our prayer takes
possession of our whole life.*
—ANDREW MURRAY

*He who has learned to pray
has learned the greatest secret of
a holy and a happy life.*
—WILLIAM LAW

*One night alone in prayer
might make us new men, changed
from poverty of soul to spiritual wealth,
from trembling to triumphing.*
—CHARLES SPURGEON

What a man is on his knees before God,
that he is—no more, and no less.
—ROBERT MURRAY MCCHEYNE

Prayer—secret, fervent,
believing prayer—lies at the root
of all personal godliness.
—WILLIAM CAREY

We become what we are called to be by praying.
—EUGENE PETERSON

Heavenly father,
I do not fully understand all the reasons
why I pray,
but what I do understand
is that you use prayer to change me.
And Lord,
I want to be changed.
Amen.

-4-
PRAYER AND ACTION

One of the constant themes of the great writers on prayer is that we must live what we pray. The words we form with our lips should be mirrored by our actions, for God desires more from us than empty talk.

It is through the act of praying that our hearts and minds are refocused, and the new priorities that arise from our times of prayer call for changes not only in our actions, but also in our attitudes and character. Through prayer we are changed and transformed, and that transformation will make us into different people than we were when we first sank to our knees.

A prayer makes sense only if it is lived.
Unless they are "lived," unless life and prayer
become completely interwoven, prayers become a
sort of polite madrigal which you offer to God at
moments when you are giving time to Him.
—ANTHONY BLOOM

He who prays as he ought,
will endeavor to live as he prays.
—JOHN OWEN

You can do more than pray
after you have prayed, but you cannot do more
than pray until you have prayed.
—S. D. GORDON

Everything that one turns
in the direction of God is prayer.
—IGNATIUS OF LOYOLA

Prayer is not merely a passive activity. We cannot use the phrase, "I prayed about it" as an excuse for inaction. Through our actions we give feet to our prayers.

*If anyone turns a deaf ear to the law,
even his prayers are detestable.*
—PROVERBS 28:9

*Dear friends, if our hearts do not condemn us,
we have confidence before God and receive from him
anything we ask, because we obey his commands
and do what pleases him.*
—I JOHN 3:21

*Work as if everything depended upon work
and pray as if everything depended upon prayer.*
—WILLIAM BOOTH

*I insist again, your foundation must not
consist of prayer and contemplation alone:
unless you acquire the virtues and practice them,
you will always be dwarfs…making no progress,
for you know that to stop is to go back—if you love,
you will never be content to come to a standstill.*
—TERESA OF AVILA

*In prayer we tempt God,
if we ask that which we labor not for.
Our endeavor must second our devotion.*
—RICHARD SIBBES

In God's eyes, our obedient and sacrificial
actions can themselves become a form of prayer.

*Every action performed in the sight of God
because it is the will of God, and in the manner
that God wills, is a prayer and indeed a better prayer
than could be made in words at such times.*
—NICHOLAS GROU

*Do not reduce your prayers to words, but rather
make the totality of your life a prayer to God.*
—ISAAC OF SYRIA

*He prayeth well, who loveth well
Both man and bird and beast
He prayeth best, who lovest best,
All things both great and small;
For the dear God who loveth us,
He made and loveth all.*
—SAMUEL TAYLOR COLERIDGE

*0, do not pray for easy lives.
Pray to be stronger men. Do not pray
for tasks equal to your powers. Pray for
powers equal to your tasks.*
—PHILLIPS BROOKS

*Prayer is not something that I do;
prayer is something that I am.*
—WARREN WIERSBE

Heavenly Father,
Let me learn from my times of prayer.
Refocus my priorities,
Rekindle my passion,
Reinvigorate my commitment.
Help me to rise from my knees
And take what I have learned with me into my
world.
Let not my words be hollow,
But give me the strength to live what I pray.
In Jesus' name,
Amen.

-5-
PREPARING YOURSELF
FOR PRAYER

Proper preparation is the key to success in many areas of life. The student who spends time in study will do better on her test than she would have done had she not reviewed and thought about the material on the exam. The marriage that is preceded by much counseling and discussion of potential problem areas is less likely to be one of the casualties that swell the divorce statistics. A sports team is more likely to gain victory if the players prepare for the game by studying the tactics and strategies of their opponents and readying themselves physically and emotionally for the contest.

It is no different with prayer. A little preparation before our time of prayer will make us less susceptible to distraction, more focused, and more spiritually prepared for intimate communion with God.

The phrase "learning to pray"
sounds strange to us. If the heart does not
overflow and begin to pray by itself we say, it
will never "learn" to pray. But it is a dangerous
error, surely very widespread among Christians,
to think that the heart can pray by itself. For then we
confuse wishes, hopes, sighs, laments, rejoicings—
all of which the heart can do by itself—with prayer.
And we confuse earth and heaven, man and God.
Prayer does not mean simply to pour out one's
heart. It means rather to find the way to God
and to speak with Him, whether the heart is
full or empty. No man can do that by himself.
For that he needs Jesus Christ.
—DIETRICH BONHOEFFER

The labor of prayer requires
a definite plan and purpose.
—O. HALLESBY

How do we prepare? The great writers offer us some advice, emphasizing that communion with God comes more easily to those who prepare themselves for it.

Our part in prayer is to try to raise our minds and hearts to God, to spend time making the effort. "Trying to pray" is prayer, and it is very good prayer. The will to try is also His gift.
— BASIL HUME

Murmuring with the mouth is easy, or looks easy. But to fill the words with the sincerity of the heart in diligent devotion, i.e., desire and faith, so that we seriously desire what the words contain and do not doubt that the prayer is heard, that is a great work in the sight of God.
— MARTIN LUTHER

The person who is about to come to prayer should withdraw for a little and prepare himself and so become more attentive and active for the whole of his prayer. He should cast away all temptation and troubling thoughts and remind himself so far as he is able, of the majesty whom he approaches, and that it is impious to approach Him carelessly, sluggishly, and disdainfully; and he should put away all extraneous things. This is how he should come to prayer, stretching out his soul, as it were, instead of his hands, straining his mind toward God instead of his eyes.
—ORIGEN

As we prepare to pray, it is essential to carefully consider any attitudes or actions that might become hindrances, such as improprieties in our relationships, pretentiousness, unconfessed sin, or an unforgiving heart.

If I had cherished sin in my heart,
the LORD would not have listened,
—PSALM 66:18

*Husbands, in the same way
be considerate as you live with your wives,
and treat them with respect…so that
nothing will hinder your prayers.*
—I PETER 3:7

*When you pray, do not be
like the hypocrites, for they love to pray
standing in the synagogues and on the
street corners to be seen by men. I tell
you the truth, they have received
their reward in full.*
—MATTHEW 6:5

*If you forgive men when they sin
against you, your heavenly Father will
also forgive you. But if you do not forgive
men their sins, your Father will not
forgive your sins.*
—MATTHEW 6:14

Searching our hearts in all these areas will cause us to see how far we are from being the kind of people God wants us to be. The result of this self-examination will be humility, the kind of humility that must be resident within our hearts for true prayer: the awareness of our limitations and our need of God.

He does not answer when men cry out
because of the arrogance of the wicked.
Indeed, God does not listen to their empty
plea; the Almighty pays no attention to it.
—JOB 35:12

The first rule of right prayer is
to have our heart and mind framed
as becomes those who are entering
into converse with God.
—JOHN CALVIN

Humility is the principal aid to prayer.
—TERESA OF AVILA

One common suggestion from the spiritual giants of the past is that we spend time reading the Scriptures in order to prepare our hearts. The Bible can be a mirror in which we see ourselves. It will reveal our imperfections, self-deceptions, and impetuousness. It will also provide us with material we can use to bring focus to our prayer time.

It is always useful to read a portion of the Scriptures before prayer, whether performed in the family or in the closet. In doing this, mark some particular passages, that they may become a subject for your petitions; by attending to this, all formality and sameness in this sacred duty will be prevented; and you will have an abundance of materials for petitions, supplications, thanksgiving, and etc. And thus your prayers will never be tedious, unsatisfactory, or unedifying, either to yourself or to others.
—ADAM CLARKE

To pray well is the better half of study.
—MARTIN LUTHER

Begin with reading or hearing.
Go on with meditation: end in prayer....
Reading without meditation is unfruitful;
to meditate and to read without prayer
upon both, is without blessing.
—WILLIAM BRIDGE

All of these actions work together to cause us to meditate on the state of our own hearts, our immense need, God's graciousness, and the promise that He is the answer to our prayers.

I will meditate on all your works
and consider all your mighty deeds.
—PSALM 77:12

Meditation is stretching the bow;
prayer is letting the arrow fly. If we are not
to miss the mark, we must not only pray
but also prepare ourselves in meditation.
— DONALD BLOESCH

My eyes stay open through the
watches of the night, that I may
meditate on your promises.
— PSALM 119:148

Let me understand the teachings
of your precepts: then I will meditate
on your wonders.
— PSALM 119:27

Father,
Teach us to be serious enough
about our prayer
That we take the time and effort
to prepare.
Guide us into prayer that will cooperate
with Your plan
And let Your word reveal to us
Both the state of our hearts and the
riches of Your grace.
Through Your son, Jesus,
Amen.

-6-

THE ART OF PRAYER

The art of prayer is best learned with the help of mentors. But what are we to do if we don't have any great pray-ers in our circle of acquaintances?

As this book has illustrated, we can find mentors among the great Christians of the past and present, people we can meet only in books. If we are to become effective pray-ers, we should look to the example of these great prayer warriors who have preceded us, men and women who accomplished so much in their lives because they gave themselves much to prayer.

They provide for us a challenge, as well as much practical advice about how to undertake the task of prayer. In their writings, they address many of the "nitty gritty" issues and offer us insights into the elements of effective prayer. What kind of help do they offer?

First, they teach us that we should pray fervently, with our whole heart:

> *He who prays fervently knows not*
> *whether he prays or not, for he is not thinking*
> *of the prayer which he makes, but of God,*
> *to whom he makes it.*
> —FRANCIS DE SALES

> *Cold prayers, like cold suitors,*
> *are seldom effective in their aims.*
> —JIM ELLIOT

> *Many pray with their lips for that*
> *for which their hearts have no desire.*
> —JONATHAN EDWARDS

*I fancy that we may sometimes be
deterred from small prayers by a sense of
our own dignity rather than God's.*
—C. S. LEWIS

*In prayer the lips ne'er act
the winning part
Without the sweet concurrence
of the heart.*
—ROBERT HERRICK

Second, they teach us that we should pray
specifically, not in generalities.

*Let your prayer be so definite
that you can say as you leave the prayer closet,
"I know what I have asked from the Father,
and I expect an answer."*
—ANDREW MURRAY

Third, they teach us that we should pray with focus, avoiding distractions. And when distractions do come, we are taught that we should not let them defeat us.

What various hindrances we meet
In coming to the mercy-seat;
Yet who, that knows the worth of prayer,
But wishes to be often there?
—WILLIAM COWPER

Thoughts continue to jostle in your head
like mosquitoes. To stop this jostling you must
bind the mind with one thought, or the thought of
One only. An aid to this is a short prayer, which
helps the mind to become simple and unified.
—THEOPHAN THE RECLUSE

I throw myself down in my Chamber,
and I call in, and invite God, and His Angels
hither. And when they are there, I neglect God
and His Angels, for the noise of a Fly, for the
rattling of a Coach, for the whining of a door;
I talk on, in the same posture of praying; eyes
lifted up; knees bowed down; as though I prayed
to God; and, if God, or His Angels should ask me,
when I last thought of God in that prayer, I cannot
tell.... A memory of yesterday's pleasures, a fear of
tomorrow's dangers, a straw under my knee, a noise
in mine ear, a light in mine eye, an any thing, a
nothing, a fang, a chimera in my brain, troubles
me in my prayer. So there is nothing, nothing in
spiritual things, perfect in this world. I turn to hearty
and earnest prayer to God, and I fix my thoughts
strongly—as I think upon Him, and before I have
perfected one petition ... the spirit of slumber
closes mine eyes and I pray drowsily.
—JOHN DONNE

*The time of business does not with me
differ from the time of prayer, and in the noise
and clatter of my kitchen, while several persons
are at the same time calling for different things, I
possess God in as great tranquility as if I were
upon my knees at the blessed sacrament.*
— BROTHER LAWRENCE

*It is indeed essential for a man to take up
the struggle against his thoughts if the veils
woven from his thoughts and covering up his
intellect are to be removed, thus enabling him
to turn his gaze without difficulty towards
God and to avoid following the will of
his wandering thoughts.*
— AMMONAS THE HERMIT

You are not the only one
troubled by wandering thoughts; our
mind constantly wanders, but the will is
mistress of our faculties and must recall it
and bring it to God as its last end.
—BROTHER LAWRENCE

If you have never had any distractions,
you don't know how to pray. For the secret
of prayer is a hunger for God and for the vision
of God, a hunger that lies far deeper than the level
of language of affection. And a man whose memory
and imagination are persecuting him with a crowd
of useless or even evil thoughts and images may
sometimes be forced to pray far better, in the
depths of his heart, than one whose mind is
swimming with clear concepts and brilliant
purposes and easy acts of love.
—THOMAS MERTON

Build yourself a cell in your heart
and retire there to pray.
—CATHERINE OF SIENNA

Fourth, they teach us to pray with simplicity, not encumbering ourselves with the quest for profundity or elaborate articulation of our needs. It is not the eloquence of our words, but the honest desire in our hearts, that is precious to God. Long-windedness is no sign of a meaningful prayer life.

Do not think to overcome the Almighty
by the best material put in the aptest phrase.
No. One groan, one sigh from a wounded
soul, excels and prevails with God.
—WILLIAM PENN

*Do not attempt to talk much when you pray
lest your mind be distracted in searching for words.
One word of the publican propitiated God, and one
cry of faith saved the thief. Loquacity in prayer often
distracts the mind and leads to fantasy, whereas
brevity makes for concentration.*
—JOHN CLIMACUS

*Those who delight in a multitude of words,
even though they say admirable things,
are empty within.*
—ISAAC OF NINEVEH

*Some men will spin out a long prayer
telling God who and what He is, or they
pray out a whole system of divinity. Some
people preach, others exhort the people, till
everybody wishes they would stop and God
wishes so, too, most undoubtedly.*
—CHARLES G. FINNEY

Prayer is not eloquence, but earnestness;
not the definition of helplessness,
but the feeling of it.
—HANNAH MORE

We ought to act with God in the
greatest simplicity, speaking to Him frankly
and plainly and imploring His assistance
in our affairs, just as they happen.
—BROTHER LAWRENCE

It may be that he can only sigh,
stammer and mutter. But as long as it
is a request brought before God, God
will hear it and understand it.
—KARL BARTH

*Do not affect to pray long, for the sake of
length, or to stretch out your matter by labor and
toil of thought, beyond the furniture of your own
spirit. God is not more pleased with prayers merely
because they are long, nor are Christians ever the
more edified. It is much better to make up by the
frequency of our devotions what we want in the
length of them, when we feel our spirits dry, and
our hearts straitened.... God has bestowed a variety
of natural, as well as spiritual talents and gifts
upon men; nor is the best Christian, or a saint
of the greatest gifts, always fit for long prayers.*
—ISAAC WATTS

*We may know for certain that we shall
be heard, not because we use many words, but
on account of the purity of our hearts and our tears
of sorrow. Our prayer, therefore, should be short
and pure, unless by some inspiration of
divine grace it be prolonged.*
—BENEDICT OF NURSIA

The fewer the words, the better the prayer.
The more words, the worse the prayer. Few words
and much meaning is Christian. Many words
and little meaning is pagan.
—MARTIN LUTHER

Countless numbers are deceived in multiplying
prayers. I would rather say five words devoutly with
my heart than five thousand which my soul does not
relish with affection and understanding.
—EDMUND THE MARTYR

Great talent is a gift of God,
but it is a gift which is by no means necessary
in order to pray well. This gift is required in order
to converse well with men; but it is not necessary
in order to speak well with God. For that, one
needs good desires, and nothing more.
—JOHN OF THE CROSS

*Converse much with your own hearts,
get well acquainted with the state of your souls,
attend to your spiritual wants and weaknesses,
frequently recollect the mercies you receive from
God, and inquire what returns you have made....
In all your prayers avoid the extremes of too mean
and too pompous a style. A pompous style shows
a mind too full of self and too little affected with
a sense of divine things.... Aim at nothing but
pouring out the soul before God in the most genuine
language.... Be not too solicitous to introduce novelties
into your prayers. Desire not to pray as nobody ever
prayed before, or will probably ever pray again.
Novelties may sometimes amuse, but in prayer
they more frequently disgust. Besides, they have
the appearance of too much art, and as new things
are generally the product of the imagination, they
are not so proper for prayer as preaching, and
even in that they must be moderate.*

—PHILLIP DODDRIDGE

Finally, those experienced in the art of prayer teach us to pray honestly, for God knows our hearts and is not fooled by our careful posturing. We do not need to pretend to have emotions or concerns that we really do not have. Conversely, we should not imagine that God will be shocked or surprised or disappointed if we put into words how we really feel. God is not afraid of the honest statement of what is in our hearts. He already knows!

God, whose knowledge is infinite,
can alone read clearly into its recesses,
and fathom its most secret foldings. He sees
our thoughts, even before we have formed them;
he discovers our most hidden paths, he views
all our stratagems and evasions.
—FRANCIS DE SALES

*Complaint against God is far nearer
to God than indifference about Him.*
　—GEORGE MACDONALD

*We must lay before Him what is in us,
not what ought to be in us.*
　—C. S. LEWIS

*If we depend too much on our
imagination and emotions, we will not
turn ourselves to God but will plunge into a
riot of images and fabricate for ourselves our
own home-made religious experience.*
　—THOMAS MERTON

When we pray, we can pray silently, in the privacy of our hearts.

Or, we can pray out loud, allowing others to hear our call unto the Lord.

There is disagreement among the prayer warriors about which is the most important. Probably the balanced life of prayer will include abundant examples of both mental and verbal prayer.

We cannot speak of God,
He is beyond compare,
And so we can adore Him
best with silent prayer.
—ANGELUS SILESIUS

When thou prayest, rather let thy heart be without
words than thy words without heart.
—JOHN BUNYAN

Pray as you think.
Consciously embrace with your heart
every gleam of light and truth that comes to
your mind. Thank God for and pray about
everything that strikes you powerfully.
—JOHN OWEN

I still think the prayer without words
is the best—if one can really achieve it. But now
I see that in trying to make it my daily bread I was
counting on a greater mental and spiritual strength
than I really have. To pray successfully without
words one needs to be "at the top of one's form."
—C. S. LEWIS

A man who prays much in private
will make short prayers in public.
—DWIGHT L. MOODY

*Prayer without words rarely satisfies
the soul. Mere mental prayer is necessarily
imperfect; earnest, fervent prayer constrains
us to express it in words.*
—ABRAHAM KUYPER

*We must consider that whoever
refuses to pray in the holy assembly
of the godly knows not what it is to pray
individually, or in a secret spot, or at home.
Again, he who neglects to pray alone in private,
however unremittingly he may frequent public
assemblies, there contrives only windy prayers,
for he defers more to the opinion of men than
to the secret judgment of God.*
—JOHN CALVIN

*The devil enjoys hearing a prayer
that is addressed to an audience.*
—UNKNOWN

Everyone has their favorite times to pray, but let's not forget that any time of the day is an appropriate time to turn to God.

*Let the day have a blessed baptism
by giving your first waking thoughts
into the bosom of God. The first hour
of the morning is the rudder of the day.*
—HENRY WARD BEECHER

*Prayer is the nearest approach to God
and the highest enjoyment of Him that we
are capable of in this life. It is as much your
duty to rise to pray as to pray when you are
risen. And if you are late at your prayers you
offer to God the prayers of an idle, slothful
worshiper who rises to prayers as idle
servants rise to their labor.*
—WILLIAM LAW

No one in his senses,
if he has any power of ordering his own day,
should reserve his chief prayers for bedtime—
obviously the worst possible hour for any
action which needs concentration.
—C. S. LEWIS

The man who says his prayers in the
evening is a captain posting his sentries.
After that, he can sleep.
—CHARLES BAUDELAIRE

Who goes to bed, and doth not pray
Maketh two nights to every day!
—GEORGE HERBERT

Many of the great writers on prayer found that it was helpful to keep a list of prayer requests to assist them in keeping focused on the needs they wished to bring before the throne of grace. The other advantage of this practice is that it allows us to keep track of the answers God brings.

What a blessed habit I have found my prayer list. Morning by morning, it takes me via the Throne of all Grace straight to the intimate personal heart of each one mentioned here, and I know that He who is not prescribed by time and geography answers immediately.
—OSWALD CHAMBERS

Andrew Murray suggests that it is a great help to find a specific place to pray, a regular spot for those quiet times with God. This can become a habitual place of meeting for times of prayer:

> *The first thing the Lord teaches His disciples*
> *is that they must have a secret place for prayer;*
> *every one must have some solitary spot where he*
> *can be alone with his God. He wants each one to*
> *choose for himself the fixed spot where He can daily*
> *meet him. That inner chamber, that solitary place is*
> *Jesus' schoolroom. That spot may be anywhere; that*
> *spot may change from day to day if we have to*
> *change our abode; but that secret place there must be,*
> *with the quiet time in which the pupil places himself*
> *in the Master's presence, to be by Him prepared to*
> *worship the Father. There alone, but there most*
> *surely, Jesus comes to teach us to pray.*
> —ANDREW MURRAY

And then, let us take what we have learned in prayer into the world by keeping our heart attuned to the spirit of prayer. Let the lovely fragrance you carry from your time in God's presence sweeten the atmosphere wherever you go.

After prayer, be careful not to agitate
your heart, lest you spill the precious balm
it has received. My meaning is, that you must,
for some time, if possible, remain in silence, and
gently remove your heart from prayer to your
other employments; retaining, as long as you
can, a feeling of the affections which
you have conceived.
—FRANCIS DE SALES

Above all, whether we pray silently or aloud, spontaneously or with prayer aids like a list, in the midst of the bustle of life or in our closet of prayer, we must stop merely talking about prayer or reading about prayer and actually begin to pray!

If you want a life of prayer,
the way to get it is by praying.
—THOMAS MERTON

Lord,
you are my teacher.
Do not let me try so hard to duplicate
the habits of others
That I neglect to keep my prayers
personal and heartfelt.
Take from me the arrogance
That would tell me I have mastered
the art of prayer,
And let me embark on the adventure
of never being satisfied.
Learning to hunger and thirst for righteousness
To strive to know you ever more intimately,
And love you with my whole being.
Amen.

-7-

TAKING UP THE CHALLENGE

The pages of this book have been filled with insights on prayer, testimonies of its effectiveness, and suggested methods that we might use to improve our prayer lives. Some of these methods and ideas might be new to you, and you may be excited about the prospect of putting them into practice. But if you approach the task with the expectation that the difficulties of prayer will be solved by learning a new technique or gaining a new perception, you will most likely be disappointed. Prayer is hard work. There is no easy shortcut to vibrant prayer.

Disappointment can also arise from thinking that every method will work for every person. But not every insight will be fruitful to every believer. Prayer is individual; as individual as your own personal relationship with God. What was helpful to one of the great writers of the past may be ineffective, unworkable, or impractical for you, no matter how much effort you expend. What is inspiring and eye-opening to one may be confusing to another. God made each of us unique, and His ways with us will be as individual as we are.

Find the way of prayer that works best for you. Often the most natural way of praying will be the best. For example, my knees tend to wear out pretty quickly, so I have found that a bracing walk outdoors creates, for me, a natural environment for prayer. But just because it is natural or easy doesn't necessarily mean it is the best path. After all, we cannot allow ourselves to become lazy when it comes to spiritual matters. It would be a mistake to let your prayers be limited by your preferences or your natural tendencies. It is a good thing to break out of your accustomed mold. By the same don't always be searching for some new wrinkle or method. At its heart, prayer is a pretty simple act. Don't muddy the waters by a search for the novel or the offbeat.

One of the best ways to improve your prayer life is by learning more about the focus of your prayers: God. Read the Scriptures to gain greater understanding of who God is and what He has done for us. Let your thinking about life be shaped by biblical truths, and consequently, your prayers as well. Our prayer lives are often limited or thrown off course by poor theological understanding, but they can be set afire when we gain deeper understanding about God's ways. If we seek God with our mind as well as our heart, new vistas of understanding will open before us and more focus will be given to our prayers.

As I look back over the pages of this book, I am reminded again of the relevance of the writings of the past for those of us who live in the present. There is much we can learn if we will bend our ears to the insights of the great saints who have preceded us. They challenge us anew not to take lightly the serious task of prayer.

But what should we do with the insights we have gained? If they remain only interesting concepts, if they do not penetrate into our hearts and challenge us, then they have failed to do their work. As Andrew Murray reminds us, prayer is something we learn by doing:

Reading a book about prayer,
listening to lectures, and talking about it
is very good, but it won't teach you to pray.
You get nothing without exercise, without practice.
I might listen for a year to a professor of music
playing the most beautiful music, but that
won't teach me to play an instrument.

Hopefully, the profound thoughts about prayer recorded in this book will help us make the choice to give ourselves to prayer, for prayer begins with a choice: We must choose to involve God in all the various aspects of our life. We won't really begin to make progress in prayer until we decide to take prayer seriously. We may need to do some rearranging of our priorities. Prayer should be one of the major priorities in the life of the believer. Sadly, it often is crowded out by the press of other activities, even our "religious" ones.

When we look into the lives of these great men and women of the past, we see a commitment to prayer. In fact, the strength and unflagging persistence of their prayer lives were such that they sometimes were referred to as the "athletes of prayer" or "prayer warriors." In the same way that an athlete will structure his or her life around the accomplishment of a desired athletic goal—running faster, hitting the ball farther, developing greater endurance, and so on—so did these athletes of prayer make prayer central to their lives. They expended themselves to become better, and more fervent, prayers. By doing so, they changed the world.

Are we willing to do the same? Are we willing to restructure our goals, our priorities, and our time around the act of serious prayer? Will we expend the necessary energy to work at becoming more focused in our prayers? Will we make times of prayer a central part of our schedule rather than something we do if we can find the extra time? Are we willing to keep on practicing, to keep on praying, even when it becomes difficult or boring, seems pointless, or seems too emotionally demanding?

All the rich and profound thoughts on prayer, that we have as a legacy from the past, are of no value to us unless they actually cause us to take prayer more seriously.

And we should take prayer seriously.

Any way we look at it, prayer is an awesome privilege. To think that the creator of all things desires to hear about all our needs and concerns is a staggering thought. Seen from an eternal perspective, the matters that concern us are, for the most part, rather trivial. Who are we that God should bother to hear us? And yet, God does not hold our concerns to be trivial. The wonder of it all is that God is willing to concern Himself with what concerns us. That He is willing, and in fact desirous, to lend an ear to our problems and struggles reveals a great deal about our relationship with Him and His love for us.

Love is God's motivation for giving us the gift of prayer. It should also be our prime motivation in praying. We do not pray primarily to receive whatever it is we think we need, or to fulfill what we perceive to be our religious duty. We pray because we love God. We pray because our hearts cry out from their need to communicate with Him. We pray because we desire His companionship with us on the pathway of life.

God is not an impersonal metaphysical force or an indifferent "supreme being." He has revealed Himself to be a lover—one who wants to be in relationship with His creatures. He is the source of all life and the giver of every good gift, even those gifts that may not seem good to us at the time we receive them. He is infinite, but He is also personal.

Prayer is the most intimate activity we can share with God. I do not think it is too much of a stretch to suggest that prayer is to our relationship with God what the sexual relationship is to a healthy marriage. It is the utmost in self-revelation, where we bare our hearts before God. In prayer we reveal our true selves and make ourselves vulnerable to God. We spend our passion in pursuing His pleasure. We long for His presence with us and in us.

As we undertake the life of prayer, then, it is important that we keep our eyes on what really matters. We should focus not on the methods of prayer, but on the One to whom we pray. A heart that pants for God as a deer pants for water (Psalm 42:1) is the foundation of true prayer. We pray because we long to be in communication with God. We want to speak, to pour out our hearts, to be heard. The glory of prayer is that we can be, in a sense, face to face with God, even as Adam was in the garden when God walked with him "in the cool of the day." Prayer truly is the pathway to the very heart of God!

-8-

FAMOUS PRAYERS AND
PRAYERS OF THE FAMOUS

Our prayers need not be beautifully articulated or theologically profound to receive an answer from God. He appreciates the honest outpourings of our heart. Our words are precious to Him. But, from those who have expressed themselves well in their praying, perhaps much more clearly than we are capable of ourselves, we can learn the discipline of thinking carefully and praying seriously.

*Come near to the holy men and women
of the past and you will soon feel the heat of
their desire after God. They mourned for Him,
they prayed and wrestled and sought for Him
day and night, in season and out, and when
they had found Him the finding was all the
sweeter for the long seeking.*
—A.W. TOZER

I have gathered together a collection of some wellknown "written" prayers, many composed by the same writers whose thoughts on prayer we have considered.

We can use these prayers as models to fashion our own prayers, inspirations to prepare our hearts to pray, or ways to give voice to concerns and feelings that we cannot articulate. We can make these prayers our own, for sometimes they will help us to express what we struggle to put into words for ourselves. When prayed with focus and concentration they can give our hearts wings to fly upward to God.

*My Lord Jesus, I beseech You, do not be far
from me, but come quickly and help me, for vain
thoughts have risen in my heart and worldly fears
have troubled me sorely. How shall I break them
down? How shall I go unhurt without Your help?
I shall go before you, says our Lord; I shall drive
away the pride of your heart, then shall I set open
to you the gates of spiritual knowledge and show
you the privacy of my secrets. O Lord, do as You
say, and then all wicked imaginings shall flee
away from me. Truly, this is my hope and my only
comfort—to fly to You in every trouble, to trust
steadfastly in You, to call inwardly upon You,
and to abide patiently Your coming and Your
heavenly consolations which, I trust,
will quickly come to me.*

—THOMAS À KEMPIS

*All things live in You, O God.
You command us to seek You, and You are
always ready to be found. To know You is life,
to serve You is freedom, to praise You is joy.
We bless and adore You, worship and
magnify You, thank and love You.*

—AUGUSTINE

Teach us good Lord, to serve Thee as Thou deservest:
To give and not count the cost;
To fight and not heed the wounds;
To toil and not to seek for rest,
To labor and not ask for reward
Save that of knowing that we do Thy will.
            —IGNATIUS OF LOYOLA

Lord, what I once had done with youthful might,
Had I been from the first true to the truth,
Grant me, now old, to do—with better sight,
And humbler heart, if not the brain of youth;
So wilt Thou, in Thy gentleness and truth,
Lead back thy old soul, by the path of pain,
Round to his best—young eyes and heart and brain.
            —GEORGE MACDONALD

Lord, open our eyes,
That we may see You in our brothers and sisters.
Lord, open our ears, That we may hear the cries
of the hungry, the cold, the frightened, the oppressed.
Lord, open our hearts, That we may love each other
as You love us. Renew in us Your spirit,
Lord, free us and make us one.
            —MOTHER TERESA

I asked for strength that I might achieve;
I was made weak that I might learn humbly to obey.
I asked for health that I might do greater things;
I was given infirmity that I might do better things.
I asked for riches that I might be happy;
I was given poverty that I might be wise.
I asked for power that I might have
the praise of men;
I was given weakness that I might
feel the need of God.
I asked for all things that I might enjoy life;
I was given life that I might enjoy all things.
I got nothing that I had asked for,
but everything that I had hoped for.
Almost despite myself my unspoken prayers
were answered;
I am, among all men, most richly blessed.
—AN UNKNOWN CONFEDERATE SOLDIER

Thou hast given so much to me
Give one thing more—a grateful heart:
Not thankful when it pleaseth me,
As if thy blessings had spare days,
But such a heart whose pulse may be
Thy Praise.
—GEORGE HERBERT

O Holy Spirit,
As the sun is full of light, the ocean
full of water, heaven full of glory, so may
my heart be full of Thee. Give me Thyself
without measure, as an unimpaired fountain,
as inexhaustible riches. I bewail my coldness,
poverty, emptiness, imperfect vision, languid
service, prayerless prayers, praiseless praises.
Suffer me not to grieve or resist Thee. Come as
power, to expel every rebel lust, to reign supreme
and keep me Thine. Come as teacher, leading me
into all truth, filling me with all understanding.
Come as love, that I may adore the Father, and love
him as my all. Come as joy, to dwell in me, move
in me, animate me. Come as light, illuminating the
Scripture, molding me in its laws. Come as sanctifier,
body, soul, and spirit wholly Thine. Come as helper,
with strength to bless and keep, directing my every
step. Come as beautifier, bringing order out of
confusion, loveliness out of chaos. Magnify to
me Thy glory by being magnified in me, and
make me redolent of Thy fragrance.
—PURITAN PRAYER

I have no wit, no words, no tears;
My heart within me like a stone
Is numbed too much for hopes or fears.
Look right, look left, I dwell alone;
I lift mine eyes, but dimmed with grief
No everlasting hills I see;
My life is in the falling leaf;
O Jesus quicken me.

My life is like a faded leaf,
My harvest dwindled to a husk;
Truly my life is void and brief
And tedious in the barren dusk;
My life is like a frozen thing.
No bud nor greenness can I see;
Yet rise it shall—the sap of Spring,
O Jesus, rise in me.

My life is like a broken bowl,
A broken bowl that cannot hold
One drop of water for my soul
Or cordial in the searching cold;
Cast in the fire the perished thing;
Melt and remould it, till it be
A royal cup for Him my King:
O Jesus drink of me.

—CHRISTINA ROSETTI

*Most merciful God, order my day
so that I may know what You want me
to do, and then help me to do it. Let me not
be elated by success or depressed by failure.
I want only to take pleasure in what pleases
You, and only to grieve at what displeases You.
For the sake of Your love I would willingly forgo
all temporal comforts. May all the joys in which
You have no part weary me. May all the work
which You do not prompt be tedious to me. Let
my thoughts frequently turn to You, that I may
be obedient to You without complaint, patient
without grumbling, cheerful without self-
indulgence, contrite without dejection, and
serious without solemnity. Let me hold
You in awe without feeling terrified of
You, and let me be an example to
others without any trace of pride.*
—THOMAS AQUINAS

*O God, early in the morning I cry to You.
Help me to pray and to concentrate my thoughts
on You; I cannot do this alone.*
—DIETRICH BONHOEFFER

Brief Biographies of Quoted Writers

AMMONAS THE HERMIT (unknown) Early church monk, desert father.

THOMAS AQUINAS (c. 1227–1274) Great medieval theologian and philosopher, prolific writer.

AUGUSTINE (345–430) Early African bishop and prolific writer.

KARL BARTH (1888–1968) Swiss theologian.

CHARLES BAUDELAIRE (1821–1867) French poet.

HENRY WARD BEECHER (1813–1887) American preacher.

BENEDICT OF NURSIA (c. 480–543) Great organizer and reformer of the monastic movement, developed Rule still in use.

DONALD BLOESCH (1928–   ) American theologian.

ANTHONY BLOOM (1914–   ) Swiss bishop and spiritual writer.

BONAVENTURE (1221–1274) Teacher and mystical theologian.

DIETRICH BONHOEFFER (1906–1945) German theologian and pastor, author of numerous books, martyred by Nazis.

WILLIAM BOOTH (1829–1912) Founder of the Salvation Army.

WILLIAM BRIDGE (1600–1670) English preacher.

PHILLIPS BROOKS (1835–1893) American minister and hymn writer.

JOHN BUNYAN (1628–1688) English writer of *Pilgrim's Progress* and other books.

JOHN CALVIN (1509–1564) French reformer and systematic theologian.

WILLIAM CAREY (1761–1834) Pioneer of the modern missionary movement.

AMY CARMICHAEL (1867–1951) English missionary to India.

CATHERINE OF SIENA (1347–1380) Mystic, church leader.

OSWALD CHAMBERS (1874–1917) Scottish Bible teacher and writer.

ADAM CLARKE (1762–1832) Methodist theologian and commentator.

JOHN CLIMACUS (579–649) Ascetic and mystical writer.

SAMUEL TAYLOR COLERIDGE (1772–1834) English poet.

WILLIAM COWPER (1731–1800) English poet.

DIONYSIUS THE AEROPAGITE (5th or 6th century) Influential mystical writer.

PHILIP DODDRIDGE (1702–1751) English church leader and writer.

JOHN DONNE (1573–1631) English poet and preacher.

FYODOR DOSTOEVSKY (1821–1881) Russian novelist.

EDMUND THE MARTYR (c. 840–870) East Anglian king and martyr.

JONATHAN EDWARDS (1703–1758) American theologian, pastor, and prolific author.

JIM ELLIOT (1927–1956) American missionary to South America and martyr.

FRANÇOIS FENÉLON (1651–1715) French mystical writer.

CHARLES G. FINNEY (1792–1875) American evangelist and writer.

FRANCIS DE SALES (1567–1622) Bishop of Geneva and mystical writer.

S. D. GORDON (1859–1936) American devotional writer.

NICHOLAS GROU (1731–1803) French mystical writer.

O. HALLESBY (1879–1961) Norwegian theologian.

GEORGE HERBERT (1593–1633) English poet and pastor.

ROBERT HERRICK (1591–1674) English poet.

BASIL HUME (1923–   ) English cardinal and spiritual writer.

IGNATIUS OF LOYOLA (1491–1556) Basque nobleman and soldier, founder of Jesuit society.

ISAAC OF NINEVEH (c. 700) Bishop of Nineveh.

JOHN OF THE CROSS (1542–1591) Spanish priest, mystic, and poet.

THOMAS KELLY (1893–1941) American theologian and devotional writer.

THOMAS À KEMPIS (1380–1471) Monastic author of *The Imitation of Christ.*

SÖREN KIERKEGAARD (1853–1855) Danish philosopher and theologian.

ABRAHAM KUYPER (1837–1920) Dutch theologian and political leader.

FRANK C. LAUBACH (1884–1974) Linguist and American missionary to the Philippines.

WILLIAM LAW (1686–1761) Cambridge don, clergyman, and author.

BROTHER LAWRENCE (c. 1605–1691) Monk and mystical writer.

C. S. LEWIS (1898–1963) English professor, prolific writer, and Christian apologist.

MARTIN LUTHER (1482–1546) German founder of the Reformation, author of numerous treatises, commentaries, and devotional books.

GEORGE MACDONALD (1824–1904) Scottish minister, novelist, and poet.

ROBERT MURRAY MCCHEYNE (1813–1843) Scottish minister.

THOMAS MERTON (1915–1968) American monk and mystical writer.

DWIGHT L. MOODY (1837–1889) American preacher-evangelist.

HANNAH MORE (1737–1833) English writer and playwright.

MOTHER TERESA (1910-1997) Yugoslavian nun and missionary to India.

ANDREW MURRAY (1828–1917) South African devotional writer.

HENRI J. M. NOUWEN (1932–1996) Belgian–American devotional writer.

ORIGEN (c. 185–254) Important early church theologian from Alexandria.

JOHN OWEN (1616–1683) English reformed theologian.

WILLIAM PENN (1644–1718) Quaker theologian.

EUGENE PETERSON (1932–   ) American pastor and writer.

J. C. RYLE (1816–1900) English bishop and writer.

CHRISTINA ROSSETTI (1830–1894) English poet.

HENRY SCOUGAL (1650–1678) Scottish devotional writer.

FULTON SHEEN (1895–1979) American bishop and broadcaster.

ANGELUS SILESIUS (1624–1677) Polish hymn writer.

CHARLES SPURGEON (1834–1892) Gifted English preacher and writer.

TERESA OF AVILA (1515–1592) Spanish mystic, writer, and church reformer.

THEOPHAN THE RECLUSE (1815–1894) Eastern Orthodox bishop and scholar.

A. W. TOZER (1897–1963) American pastor and devotional writer.

ISAAC WATTS (1674–1748) English pastor and prolific hymn writer.

WARREN WIERSBE Contemporary American pastor and spiritual writer.

Terry Glaspey is an editor and an author of several significant books, including *Your Child's Heart, Not a Tame Lion: The Spiritual Legacy of C. S. Lewis,* and *Great Books of the Christian Tradition*. He lives in Eugene Oregon.